The Day After
Hank Williams' Birthday

Acknowledgments

Thanks to the editors and publishers of the following publications in which some of these pieces first appeared: *Hitching: Tales from the Byways and Superhighways; City of Ukiah Activities & Recreation Guide; Ukiah Library Friends Newsletter; Memo; Ace's Web World; Insomniacathon On-Line.*

Thanks to Dean McClain and Rob Zoschke for reading and commenting on early drafts of this book, G. Kent and Michael Riedell for proofreading, Carl Brush for excellent editorial suggestions, Hal Zina Bennett for design expertise and professionalism, Ace Toscano for web savvy and generosity, and Mary Miller and Nate Barth for love and support.

The Day After
Hank Williams' Birthday

Prose Pieces & Poems

Dan Barth

Secret Goldfish Press

ISBN-13: 978-0615931609
ISBN-10: 061593160X

Secret Goldfish Press
1001 Recreation Road
Ukiah, CA 95482
bookem@pacific.net

This book may be ordered from the publisher, through booksellers, or online at createspace.com or amazon.com.

This book is dedicated to the memory of my dad, Bill Barth, and his two brothers, my uncles Tubby and Bob Barth. Their wisdom, humor and music are always with me.

Contents

Jesus Sent Me

Two years in a row—this was in the late 1970s—I hitched out to Washington in the fall, then south through Oregon and California before heading back to Kentucky in time for Christmas. The first year, on the last leg of the trip, I hitched a ride from Little Rock to Louisville with a Jesus freak in a red Ford Pinto.

"Jesus told me to drive to Fort Worth," he told me. "Then when I got to Fort Worth he told me to turn right around and drive back to Louisville."

I hung on to my seat. But that was about as weird as it got, and he wasn't a bad driver, so I figured what the hell, a ride's a ride. And we arrived alive.

The next year I had made it as far as Nashville on a chilly Christmas Eve, just hitching and hoping for the best, when the same little red Pinto pulled over, same guy driving.

After the car heater got me thawed a bit, I said, "Do you remember me? You picked me up hitching once before, about a year ago."

"I sure do remember you."

"You told me then that Jesus told you where to drive."

"Yep. That's right."

"Still true?"

"You bet. This time he told me to drive from Louisville to Nashville. Then when I got to Nashville he told me to drive to Memphis. When I got to Memphis he told me to turn around and drive back to Louisville."

"Does Jesus ever tell you why he wants you to drive to these places?"

"Sometimes he does. Mostly I just take it on faith."

"What about this time? Was there any reason why you were supposed to drive to Nashville and Memphis and then back to Louisville?"

"Yep."

He looked right at me for a long moment, with a grin on his face and a gleam in his eye. And I have to admit, what he said next gave me the shivers. It was just one word: "You."

Loud Motorcycle Guy
(Zen and the Art of Motorcycle Tolerance)

This happened in July of 1995 when we were living quietly in Talmage, California, across the Russian River from Ukiah, just up the road from the Sagely City of 10,000 Buddhas.

These people moved in next door. Up all night. Cars in and out at all hours. Welfare mothers make better lovers, and like that. *All* like that. You know the kind of people I'm talking about.

With two kids. Special Needs kids. You bet. Carmine and Shannon. Playing and yelling with the little girl who rides her bike with her dress hiked up. Future draft choice, as Kelly used to say. So. . . . like that.

And about the 1st of July this motorcycle guy shows up—the mother's brother no doubt, or some old boyfriend, with his girlfriend, both tall and skinny in leathers on the bike. Speed freaks, or I miss my guess. Up all night every night—working on the bike. Out in the driveway just across the fence. Hammering. Tinkering. Carrying. Dropping. Snorting. Cursing. LOUD. For days and nights on end. Fucking motorcycle maintenance.

Fuck motorcycle maintenance. I'm trying to rest. I'm trying to read. I'm trying to get some sleep. But no. Motorcycle maintenance. At all hours. For days. And nights. On end.

Finally one night I got fed up. I came home from work at 11:15 and at 11:30 the jerk started up that goddamned out-of-tune loud motorcycle again.

I went over there. It was LOUD.

I said, "HEY!"

Above the LOUD sound of the bike I shouted, "HEY!"

He heard me.

He turned off the bike.

I said, "Are you planning on working on that much longer tonight? You're bothering people over here."

And the guy said, "What time is it?"

I said, "Eleven-thirty."

And he said, "What day is it?"

I said, "Thursday."

And he said, "Okay."

I repeated, "Are you planning on working on that much longer tonight?"

And he said, "No."

I think we understood each other. Though on my way back to our door I could swear I heard someone muttering something like "asshole" this and "fucking asshole" that. But I ignored it.

But the kicker was, just as I was walking in the door, the welfare mother wandered out of her house in her usual daze, and I heard her say, in a wondering tone, "Did someone just yell?"

Ode to My Branch Loppers

They come ready to my hand,
Like a ball bat or tennis racket,
Useful, overlooked, underrated tool—
Branch loppers.
Coupled with a bow saw, or chain saw,
They enable many things.
Downed wood, limbs and branches
Ignored by others as too troublesome,
To me become fuel for woodstove.
Branch loppers in one hand,
Bow saw in the other,
Back along the Russian River,
Mid-November, my old beat invaluable
Green and white side-step, slide-door
1969 VW van nearby,
I more than happily take over
Someone else's abandoned brush pile—
Oak wood, pine, madrone, cedar and alder.
No discriminator, my branch loppers accept it all,
Lop, lop, lop it clean
For bow saw to turn into transportable lengths.
I breathe deep. A hawk is flying.
The river flows—so far below flood stage now
It's hard to believe what it can sometimes do.

The next day I go
Up a nearby hillside after manzanita.
Manzanita tends to die out for some reason.
I don't know why.
A botanist or forester could explain it perhaps.
Or a Google search.
All I know is some stay alive and healthy
While others die, become brittle, break off, uproot.
My bow saw and branch loppers
Work on the gnarly dead manzanita.
I love the texture and color of it—
Smooth maroon turning to rough black.
Over the hillside the sawed branches go,
As close to the van as I can toss them.
I do more lopping and sawing on the flat,
And carry a good load back.

That very night,
By the airtight woodstove,
Watching through the glass,
Warmed by wine, woodfire, friendship,
I give thanks, propose a toast.
Here's to you, branch loppers,
Purchased at Ace Hardware
For less than thirty bucks—
Sharp, well-made, useful.
Long may you lop!

Ode to My Bow Saw

Soft shape
sharp teeth
half moon queen
of my tool shed
bow saw
I love you

I admit
it wasn't
love at first sight
in my younger days
using too-small bow saws
reward never equaled effort
but then I discovered
the perfect size
30-inch blade
crafted to my capabilities
designed for my desires
and ever since
I have been
in bow saw heaven

Our dog Scout
sees me pick up the bow saw
she's as happy as I am
we're heading for the woods
a cool October day

after wayward branches of oak
ones that hang too low
ones that have died out
ours for the taking
bow saw goes to work
time ceases to exist
we see what we can saw
we saw what we see sawable
yes we're having fun
useful practical fun
which contributes
to the health
and economy
of the household

Bow saw!
I thank you
for all that you enable
ambidextrous tool
there's no reason
not to use
and keep on using you

And I don't want
to forget to mention
how wonderfully quiet you are
unlike those admittedly useful
but obnoxiously loud
chainsaws

you do your work
quietly
efficiently
accurately
in a graceful
unassuming
timely manner
always without complaint

Please let me know
if there's ever anything
I can do for you

Interstate Commerce

I was hitching through St. Louis to St. Charles, Missouri in late September one year, trying to get to the home of my friends the Grundhausers. About dusk I was walking, hitching, wishing for a ride, when, of all things, a Winnebago pulled over. I ran up to it thinking maybe it was a mistake. Probably they had just pulled over to change drivers. But when I looked in the passenger-side door, the driver motioned for me to get in the back.

I climbed in and encountered a woman. Not a young woman. Not a good-looking woman. But in truth a scantily-clad woman. She was wearing a frilly lacey little pink teddy. She must have been in her late thirties—short, chubby, bad teeth, frizzy dirty-blonde hair.

The driver was a thin, middle-aged man with thinning brown hair. He looked back once, then pulled a curtain separating the cab from the back of the Winnebago.

And of course I was thinking—*What the hell is going on here?*—when the woman looked at me and said, "You wanna git some?"

Her meaning, as they say, was unmistakable.

"No-o-o thanks," was my reply.

So she shouted to the front, "No go, Harry."

The driver immediately pulled over, opened the curtain, looked at me and said, "This is as far as you go, partner."

"Oh, man, my exit's only a few more miles. Can't you just drop me there?"

"Nope. Out you go."

I had to walk the final three miles to my friends' house, but at least I had a good story to tell when I got there.

Old Franz's Hippie Tales *is a collaboration between the late great Franz Cilensek and myself. The stories are things that happened to Franz or that he knew about. He talked; I recorded, transcribed, edited and created the frame tale. The beginning of the tales is presented here.* ~db

Old Franz's Hippie Tales

by Dylan Zimmerman Jones

When I was a kid growing up in the '80s, Old Franz used to come over to our house and hang out with my mom and dad. They would fill an old water pipe, light it and pass it around. Then they would usually start telling stories about the '60s, a glorious time when they were young and anything was possible.

I am the youngest of six kids and my parents had been heavily into '60s rock, as you might guess by my name and the names of my siblings: Janis Joplin Jones, Jimi Hendrix Jones, John Lennon Jones, Joan Baez Jones, and Jim Morrison Jones. By the time I came along I guess they had run out of J names.

All of us kids used to like to hear Old Franz tell his stories about the old days. Sometimes Mom and Dad would go out and let him babysit us. Then we would do our best to get him talking and telling stories, which usually wasn't hard to do. One night he told us the story of

How Acid Ike Got His Nickname

When I lived in Berkeley in the '60s [Old Franz began], one of the guys on the scene was a little quiet longhair we all called Acid Ike. He was part of the crowd who hung around Bill Miller's store, The Store, on Telegraph Avenue. Bill Miller was quite a character, a huge guy, about 6'6" or 6'7", and not just tall but BIG. And he had a humongous beard that came down to about the middle of his chest. He took up a lot of space, both physically and psychically. Miller was always running for mayor or city council, but his store was a sort of underground supply depot stocked with old Salvation Army type goods. He had all kinds of stuff piled up in there--old buttons, fur coats, anything velvet. He was a major supplier to the Berkeley underground style. He also carried army surplus gas masks and hard hats that people could put on during riots and civil disturbances, which were frequent in those days.

Acid Ike was part of Miller's circle. He was a skinny kid, originally from Nebraska, where he used to make a living painting carnival rides at a big warehouse where they were stored during the winter. He was disheveled looking, a Dostoevskian kind of character. In Berkeley he painted murals in bars and on the sides of buildings, a talented guy.

Ike was one of those people who had an affinity for LSD. I think most of the time I ever saw him or spoke to him he was high. And he never seemed to have a bad trip. So he was always invited by various people who were mixing up batches of acid and putting it in capsules—capping parties they were called. Later on more people had machines for making it into pills, but at this time it was mostly capsules. One of the beauties of a capping party was that, although you did a lot of work, you would get higher than a kite just from handling the stuff. It would soak in through your skin pores and even the mucous membranes so that you could get high just from breathing the air. So you usually needed at least a couple of shifts.

One time one of the dealers had one of those New Testaments they used to hand out on street corners. I don't know if it was the Gideons or what, but they always had green covers. This guy liked Ike and one day, as a token of gratitude for his exceptionally good work at a capping party, presented him with this New Testament after placing a drop of liquid LSD on each page. After that Ike was always packing his New Testament. If he started to come down he would just rip out another page of Matthew, Luke, Colossians or Ephesians and chew on it for a while.

One day, in a blissed-out state, Ike wandered into a riot up in the business district of Berkeley, near University and Shattuck. Before he knew what was happening he had been rounded up with a bunch of other people and taken off to Santa Rita Prison. They all got two weeks incarceration for their misdeeds. But they let Ike keep his Bible, thinking he was a religious person.

So Bill Miller comes to me one day and says, "We gotta go out to Santa Rita and pick up some people who are being released today. You want to come along?"

I said, "Sure," and we got in Miller's van and drove out to there to pick up some of the individuals associated with the Miller conspiracy to overthrow the established order. When it came Ike's turn, the guard led him out, pushed him at us contemptuously, and said, "Here, take this little son of a bitch. He doesn't even know he's being punished." And it was true. Ike had spent the whole time eating his New Testament, tripping on Jesus.

Well, kids [Franz concluded], that's the story of how Acid Ike got his nickname. Now, may the Baby Jesus shut your mouths and open your minds.

Pig Fucker
for Old Franz

Franz said he didn't have
a highly developed vocabulary
of invective. But as usual
he was too modest.
"Pig fucker" was the line
he settled on, and I have since
found pig fucker to be a very useful
all-purpose epithet.

Stupid pig fucker!
Goddamn pig fucker!
Fuck you, you fucking pig fucker!
Impeach Bush and all the other
clueless frat boy pig fuckers in Washington.
Put down your cell phone and drive,
you air-headed pig fucker.
That long-winded pedantic pig fucker
does not have a clue that he
is boring the whole class to tears.
I have had enough of those inconsiderate
pig fucker neighbors and their
constantly barking pig fucker dogs.
I can't believe those ignorant
pseudo-patriotic pig fuckers on the hill
with their arrogant illegal

pig fucker flagpole.
How many pig fuckers does it take
to change a light bulb?
Fuck them. I hope the fucking
pig fuckers freeze to death in the dark.

Thank you, Franz. Pig fucker
has served me well and continues
to serve me in my encounters with
all the pig fuckers of the world.
People who are offended by this poem?
Like I care! Those pig fuckers
don't know poetry from pig shit.

guilty of everything
*with lines stolen from Herbert Hunke
and Dan Wakefield*

i row my boat along the muddy shore
next to the veterans bar & grill on first avenue
around the corner from where i used to live
listening to a chorus of doo-wah doo-wah
that reminds me of a plaintive dirge

there's a man there
someone from my grandfather's time
or someone i've seen in a dream
he wears a grey gabardine suit
with vest and watch chain
and walks with a wooden crookneck cane
i don't know him
but i would swear his first name is Jules
and his last name Kuilt or Guilt

this is Guilt himself
walking in a well-lit building on the muddy shore
not furtively or surreptitiously but openly
as if waiting for someone who seeks audience
to appease him, to bear him gifts

the wind shifts and i shift my oars
back water trying to float motionless
suspended in observation only mode

but the wind has other ideas
my oars splash the murky brown

and i glide away from Guilt
surprised to find myself in clearer waters

there may be no respite, nepenthe
ad astra per aspera, river lethe
there is no fucking balm in gilead
but I'll keep on, alternately rowing, drifting—
seeking a sail, clear skies, vision

TV or Not TV

All day today I was thinking I should have killed my tv last night at halftime of the Duke-Carolina game. But I didn't, so I was hoping tonight's U of L-Notre Dame game would validate my inaction. After that debacle I just gave up. Later I happened to be flipping channels and caught Jakob Dylan with Elvis Costello on the Sundance Channel, so now tv is alright with me again.

I have to admit my life has been immeasurably enriched by television. If not for tv I would not know by heart the Mr. Ed theme song or the Addams Family theme song or the Gilligan's Island theme song, or "Stairway to Gilligan's Island." Plus I would have missed seeing Hank Aaron on Kaptain Kangaroo (not to mention Mr. Green Jeans and Grandfather Clock and Bunny Rabbit and Dancing Bear and Tom Terrific and Mighty Manfred his wonder dog). I would not have seen Bill Mazeroski hit a home run to win the 1960 World Series or Ted Williams hit a home run in his last Major League at bat, or heard Dizzy Dean say to Pee Wee Reese, "Watch the microphone for me willya padnah while I grab us a couple of cold Falstaffs."

I would not have seen Heidi or the Heidi game. Would not have seen Ruby shoot Oswald or men walk on the moon while playing poker at Joe

Hipwell's house. Or heard Robert Frost recite a poem at the Kennedy inauguration.

Also how about the Beatles on Ed Sullivan and Topo Gigo on Ed Sullivan and the guy who kept all the plates spinning at the same time with Hoss and Ben and Adam and Little Joe on the other channel?

Donna Reed. Ozzie and Harriet. Father Knows Best. Danny Thomas. I watched all those shows. I watched December Bride and Our Miss Brooks. And of course Disney's Wonderful World of Color—Davy Crockett, the Swamp Fox, flubber, the sneaky Mooch play, Frankie and Annette, Mickey Mouse Club. And Buffalo Bob and Clarabelle the Clown and Howdy Doody.

There were two local kids' shows in Louisville when I was growing up there.

Funny Flickers featured Uncle Ed seated at a big tree stump in the Magic Forest with his duck friend Sylvester and a little statue man named Tom Foolery. Uncle Ed showed cartoons and Little Rascals episodes and signed off with, "So long like a hot dog, see you 'round like a donut."

For T Bar V Ranch kids dressed in cowboy outfits, came to the studio on their birthdays and were on the show. Yes, I drew my guns with Randy Atcher and Cactus Tom Brooks. And I can still sing the theme song from that one too. "Howdy, howdy boys and girls it's T Bar V Ranch Time/ We're glad to have you all aboard, we hope you're feeling fine. . ."

Saturday mornings from out of the blue of the western sky it was Sky King and Rin Tin Tin, Fury, Roy Rogers and Dale Evans and their horses Trigger and Buttermilk.

Well, okay. I wax nostalgic. You get the picture.

I saw a rerun of Petticoat Junction the other night. Bobbie Joe is still a babe.

Really I read at night mostly, but when I'm tired I watch tv. The only show I plan to watch these days and know what time it comes on is Medium. It stars Patricia Arquette as a lady who dreams things that help the Phoenix PD solve crimes. She is a beautiful dreamer and it's a good show.

Some evenings Mary and I watch Jeopardy at 7 o'clock and switch to Friends reruns during commercials. Is it just me or is Friends getting better in reruns and Seinfeld getting worse? Also have you noticed how long it is between the end of Double Jeopardy and the clue for Final Jeopardy? It's like five minutes of commercials.

Tonight's tv trivia question. Who was the original host of Jeopardy? And who was the announcer? No Googling now. Just tell me if you know.

Load up your truck and move to Beverly.

Take Manhattan, just give me that countryside.

Get your kicks on Route 66.

Head 'em up, move 'em out.

There's the signpost up ahead.

Warning, danger!

Beam me up, Scotty.

With Rose Marie and Morey Amsterdam.

David Janzen as the Fugitive.

And Jerry Mathers as the Beaver.

Satellite TV

M y son wanted to get satellite tv. My wife wanted it. I wanted it, too. So, Saturday morning I drove to the Pear Tree Shopping Center, bought a cup of coffee at Starbucks®, and walked to Radio Shack® to sign up for Dish Network®.

I have never been much of a fan of Radio Shack®. I remember the first few times I bought something there the sales clerk always wanted way more information than seemed necessary.

"One twelve-volt battery. That'll be eighty-eight cents."

"Here's a dollar."

"Okay. Your change is twelve cents. I'll just need your name, age and zip code."

"What?"

"Name, age and zip code."

"Why?"

"It's just company policy."

"Why?"

"Just is."

So to get my twelve cents and get out of there I'd give the clerk my name, age and zip code. But it did turn me off to Radio Shack®, so I rarely go there.

But this time I figured what the hell—kid, wife, satellite tv, costs the same as cable and we don't even get good reception on some channels. So, okay. Family of the future! Satellite tv!

The sales clerk at Radio Shack® was not completely up on all the latest Dish Network® deals and "packages." So while I completed the initial paperwork—name, address, phone number and credit card info—he called the special Radio Shack® direct to Dish Network® phone number and said something like, "This is Wardell, Radio Shack clerk number 82 at store number 407." He then asked a few questions about prices and packages and relayed the answers to me.

It sounded pretty good—45 dollars a month, no taxes on top of that, no hidden costs, just need a major credit card. So I said okay and Radio Shack® clerk number 82 handed me the phone.

I said hello and a voice said, "Hi, Mr. Barth, this is Ray with Dish Network®. I just need to verify your information."

"Okay."

He verified my name, address, phone number, credit card information, and "package." Then he said, "I'll need your social."

"My social?"

"Yes sir, we require a social for all packages now."

"You mean you want my social security number?"

"That's right."

"Why do you need my social security number?"

"It's just company policy."

"I'm not really comfortable with giving you my social security number. You have my credit card number."

"Yes sir, but just because you have a credit card doesn't mean you have good credit."

By now I was somewhat puzzled and taken aback, so by way of stalling a bit and collecting myself I said, "What did you say your name was?"

"Ray."

"Ray what?"

"Ray Owens."

"Where are you located, Ray?"

"In the Southwest."

"The southwestern United States."

"Yes."

"Where in the Southwest?"

"Texas."

"Where in Texas?"

"West Texas."

"Where in West Texas. What town or city?"

"El Paso."

"Ah."

There was a pause. We were both silent for a moment, then I said, "Hey, Ray?"

"Yes, sir?"

"What's your social?"

"Excuse me?"

"I'd like you to tell me your social security number."

"Sir, please hand the phone back to the clerk."

"Just a second Ray. I have one more question. Do you know the song, 'I'm proud to be an asshole from El Paso' "?

"Sir . . . "

"No??? Well hold on, I'll sing a little bit of it for you! I'M PROUD TO BE AN ASSHOLE FROM EL PASO ! ! ! ! !"

At this point three Radio Shack® clerks converged on me. I surrendered the phone, grabbed my paperwork and retreated to the sidewalk outside the store.

So there you have it—same old Radio Shack® karma. I drove home and told wife and kid the bad news. Wife was understanding. Kid was disappointed, but I said Monday I would try Direct TV®.

"Why not today?" kid wanted to know, but I said I'd had enough satellite tv for one day.

Ode to My Dad

Ron Epstein tells me
he's heading to Kentucky
to Gethsemani for a
Buddhist Catholic dialogue
and that reminds me of my Dad
who used to go on retreats
at Gethsemani
the Kentucky Catholic monastery
where Thomas Merton used to live
Dad was a member of the
Holy Name Society
at St. Pius X Church
in the Hikes Point/Bon Air
neighborhood of Louisville
the Holy Name Society
was a men's group at the church
they used to get together to
drink beer and do work
around the church and school grounds
Father Fultz was pastor of St. Pius X
in those days old Fr. Fultz
who used to call all the ladies Grandma
no matter how old they were
and when things went wrong said
"I shoulda been a plumber."

Fr. Fultz never tried to scare us with
mortal sins
and eternal damnation
like some of the nuns did
those nuns
the Sisters of Charity of Nazareth
were a combat outfit
one day I saw a small nun
Sister Mary Nicholas
punch out one of the big 8th grade boys
he was chewing tobacco
until her repeated blows to his stomach
caused him to swallow it
boy he was sick then
and of course they had their
Blues Brothers yardsticks
for palm and knuckle rapping

Fr. Fultz was much gentler
and so was my Dad
a good man if there ever was one
he and my Mom sang in the Sunday choir
and sang all the time at home
we were a happy family
we lived on Rio Rita Avenue
and Mom's name was Rita
Dad used to sing
"Rio Rita
life is sweeta

Rita
when you are near."

Dad was personnel manager
for Frankfort Distillery
out in Shively
he was on their bowling team
I still remember the beautiful
Four Roses bowling shirt
he used to wear
and going with him to
Thelmal Lanes in Shively
he threw a 16-pound ball
Mother had her own ball too
it was lighter
13 or 14 pounds

Dad coming home from work
was a big event every day
when we were real little
all of us kids
Phil Danny Barby Brian
used to hide behind the curtains
"Daddy's coming home!"
"Let's hide."
"Do you see him yet?"
"There he is!"
we'd hide
where we knew he could find us

he'd say "Now where is everybody?
Where could those darn kids be?"
and we'd giggle
then he'd find us and squeeze us
it was great to know Dad loved us
was always coming home to us
in the evenings we'd wrestle on the floor
he was big and strong
but he never hurt us
he knew what he was doing
on Sunday morning we'd all
lie in bed together
and he'd read us the funny papers
Beetle Bailey by Mort Walker
Blondie by Chic Young
L'il Abner by Al Capp
and all the rest

all these memories
because Ron Epstein
happened to mention
Gethsemani
the old Trappist monastery
out near Bardstown
Dad told us
when he went there
with the other members
of the Holy Name Society
they wouldn't talk for two days

we found that hard to believe
but he said it was true
and he'd bring home jams and jellies
made by the monks at Gethsemani

the Holy Name Society
would get together again
the next Saturday
to get the parish softball field
ready for the season
"Hit 'em where they ain't"
Dad would say
and then they'd drink beer

The Moon Was Made of Green Cheese

Summer nights on Rio Rita
Dad and Mother would sit outside
and Phil Danny Barby Brian Karen
would be outside too

Kids would come
from all over the neighborhood
Bobby and Bernie Beck would come
and Bobby and Tommy Blincoe
Mike and Amy Slavin
Charlie and Jane Blady
Bruce and Janet McCoy
Steve and Mark Taylor
Linda and Lloyd Fetzer
Jerry and Barry Keltner
(and their beagles Tramp and Drummer)

More kids would come
Dad would make up names for them
Bobby Beck became Mark One
Charlie Blady became Horse Farm Blady
Mother would laugh, Dad would kid
and tell the littlest Beck girl—
"Don't you blink those big blue eyes at me"

Dusk would fall
Lights would come on in Farnsley Park

Bats would fly eating bugs
Sometimes we'd see a searchlight
from Bowman Field
One night we saw the Northern Lights

But mainly we'd play
We'd play Catchers and Hide & Seek
and Run Sheepy Run
We'd play Dropped My Handkerchief
yesterday yesterday yesterday
We'd play Mother May I and Simon Says
and Red Light Green Light—
1, 3, 5, 7, 9, 11 green light
1, 3, 5, 7, 9, 11 red light
We'd play Tag—you're it!
We'd play Red Rover Red Rover

Dad got a huge kick out of it
Mother loved to watch us play
summer nights Louisville
Bon Air
Rio Rita
Farnsley Park
long ago

The moon was made of green cheese
I can't complain
with memories like these
still available to my aging brain

Fishing, Fathers Day

beer, cigar
drowning a worm
watching my bobber
ripples on the pond
blues, greens
browns, yellows
greys, oranges
reflected
in a bowl below the world's cares

renoir monet seurat
came close
but never quite captured this

this is what my brother—
my brother brian
who died in a car crash
when he was twelve—
this is what he loved
more than anything
it was never really about catching fish
it was the teeming life of the pond
that continually fascinated him
the myriad minnows in the shallows
multicolored multishaped wonders
orange dragonflies
black-and-white-winged dragonflies

small blue dragonflies mating in flight
yellow mustard blooming magnificently
purple sage purple
whatever that fragrant flower is
fronds of pondside algae
glint of sunlight on ripples
the wind in the reeds
the wind in the willows
the wind in the sedge
at the edge of the pond
the ephemeral nature of all phenomena

whoah! now an osprey
splashes down
ascends empty-taloned
hovers flies on alertly watching
blackbirds flit and dip
not redwinged blackbirds just—
black
a killdeer kee-kee-ka-kees
a belted kingfisher
starts to alight nearby
thinks better of it
cries as he flies away
three ducks glide in and land
at the other end of the pond
joining the four ducks
already swimming there

i cast again
find a shady spot
watch my bobber
smoke my backwoods smoke
drink my redhook ale

if i happen to catch any fish
it will be a tremendous bonus

To a Diving Duck

O to be a diving duck
And live in all the worlds
The world above
The world below
The world afloat
The world of solid earth

To fly
Like a kite on summer day
Like Superman, up up and away
Like Orville and Wilbur Wright,
uncertainly
Like Icarus, but successfully

To float
Like a cork upon the sea
Like a sailboat in a breeze
Like a leaf upon a pond
Like a buoy in a bay

To dive
Like Captain Nemo in *Nautilus*
Like Mike Nelson on *Sea Hunt*
Deep after fish or other food
Burst to the surface far away
And paddle like a pedal boat
At summer camp on holiday

To rest
At end of day on bank or berm
Or warm mud by the shore
Trade stories and jokes with other ducks
And laugh myself to sleep

Quack   Quack   Quack   Quack   Quack

The Day After Hank Williams' Birthday

It's the day after Hank Williams' birthday and you're sitting at the kitchen table after breakfast and a song starts to run through you and the song goes:

> *Move it on over*
> *Move it on over*
> *Move over little dog*
> *'Cause the big dog's movin' in.*

It's the day after Hank Williams' birthday. He would have been 90 this year if he had not died before he hit 30. You are waterproofing the front deck and a song starts running through your head and the song goes:

> *You're my gal and I'm your feller*
> *Dress up in your frock of yeller*
> *I'll look swell but you'll look sweller*
> *Settin' the woods on fire.*

It's the day after Hank Williams' birthday. He would have been 90 this year if he hadn't died on January 1, 1953 from too much morphine and whiskey in the back seat of his Cadillac on the way from Knoxville, Tennessee to Canton, Ohio. You

41

pumped up the low tire on the riding mower and got the leaf-catcher attachment out of the shed and put it on and started the mower. Now you're picking up leaves and a song starts vibrating through you and the song goes:

> Goodbye Joe, me gotta go, me oh my oh
> Me gotta go pole a pirogue down the bayou
> My Yvonne the sweetest one, me oh my oh
> Son of a gun we'll have big fun on the bayou

It's the day after Hank Williams' birthday. Hank is still well-remembered 60 years after his death. He wrote 125 songs in the time allotted to him, though some say he only wrote two—a fast one and a slow one. They all have different lyrics though, and the lyrics are great. You are sitting around watching the Giants vs. Rockies baseball game on tv and a song starts running in your head and the song goes:

> I got a hot rod Ford and a two dollar bill
> And I know a spot right over the hill
> There's soda pop and the dancin's free
> So if you wanna have fun come along with me

It's the day after Hank Williams' birthday in the year most of us have agreed to call 2013. The world situation is a mess—most of us agree on that too. The world is an incredible mix of very pleasant pleasurable beautiful lovely things and very ugly violent sordid horrible things. Hank Williams knew the world and walked in it and drove and wrote and sang and loved and drank. His son went on to become a musician and his daughter and grandson did too. You are sitting around, shank of the evening, sipping a bourbon and ginger ale, working the New York Times Sunday crossword puzzle and a clue suggests a song, which starts running through your head, and the song goes:

> *No matter how I struggle and strive*
> *I'll never get out of this world alive*

Yeah, no matter how you struggle and strive, you'll never get out of this world alive.

The Missing Bottle of Rum

A week or so ago I wanted to make a Cuba Libre, as I am wont to do after reading certain passages in novels by Ernest Hemingway, Elmore Leonard or Randy Wayne White. I had limes. I had ice. I had cola. I had tumblers (but no dancing girls). And no rum!

"What happened to my bottle of rum?" I wondered plaintively.

The leading suspects early on were Erin and Nate. Erin had just finished housesitting for us for ten days while we were in Kentucky. And Nate is seventeen years old. But Nate swears it wasn't him or any of his friends who took it. And Erin claims he doesn't drink.

Slowly but inevitably the finger of suspicion began to waggle in a direction it likely should have pointed to begin with—toward the Viking Hillbilly Apocalypse Revue.

A near no-brainer, Watson. Round up the usual derelicts.

To be more specific:

One evening a few nights after I discovered the rum was missing, I said to Mary, "Wait a minute! I haven't seen that bottle of rum since before the Viking Hillbillies were here."

And she said, "Who do you think took it, Michael or David?"

And I said, "David."

"I think Michael," she said, "but they're both good suspects."

The Viking Hillbilly Apocalypse Revue was a traveling troupe of poets, artists and musicians who visited us in Northern California on two different occasions, stayed at our place and performed at local venues. Members included Kentucky poet Ron Whitehead, Icelandic musician Michael Pollock, Kentucky artist and musician Andy Cook, Kentucky songbird Sarah Elizabeth Burkey, Kentucky poet Dean McClain (with his shotgun full of Jesus), Kentucky musician Tyrone Cotton, Kentucky artist and writer David Minton and New Jersey poet Frank Messina. They were a wild bunch, a hilarious handful of houseguests. The good times flowed like red wine.

One of my best memories of the music and poetry festivities is of an afternoon, an ordinary Friday afternoon. I got home from work and there were David and Dean sitting on stumps by the campfire pit. They looked so peaceful and content sitting there that all I wanted to do was get my clothes changed and sit out there with them. But things happened, as they tend to do, and by the time I made it to the fire circle they had moved on to another location—probably the garage to continue the Ping-Pong wars.

Often since then, though, as I walk past the fire circle, or sit there awhile, I think of David and Dean and wonder at the lovely spirit that seemed to possess them that late-May afternoon.

And now I think I know its inspiration.

Those sons-of-bitches had just finished my bottle of rum.

New Orleans 2010

1.
Flying In

that magical musical
muddy misty
old Mississippi
moseying, meandering
on down to New Orleans

wonderful warm
brown water widening
as it wanders
down to the Gulf

lush green vegetation
caressed within
the serpentine coils
of the river

ripples on the surface
barges in tow
all along the levee
roads and people go

pine trees rising
out of swamps
and greens

like you've never seen

you can hear the gumbo sound
there's music all around

2.
Olde Town Inn

I can see the umbrellas
hear the rain
clock on the wall
old round
thermometer on the wall
plates and trivets
candelabra
framed prints
old-fashioned wire
cooking accoutrements
on the wall above
the coffee pots
people talking
jazz music on the radio
bees n' beads
beads n' bees
beads and bees
in the trees

pretty red-haired girl

in long peasant skirt
and black t-shirt
  carrying two
      cups o' coffee
  back to the room
    in the morning

              3.
        On the Street

      it keeps on happening
    like this
up in the morning
      among friends
      cup o' coffee
      conversation
  books, reading
        out for a walk
all through the vieux carre
      walking, walking
the rhythm of the street
        the people
all shapes and colors
white, black, brown, tan
        olive-skinned
    girls in t-shirts
        long dark hair
      or short kinky

          breasts bounce
       nice ass in blue jeans
         on the sidewalk
     outside the Maple Leaf
     Rebirth Brass Band
            you bet
        all the people
     clasping hands, embracing
         shoulder bump
       "How *you* been?"
      "Well look who it is!"
      "Old Benjamin himself!"
     "Oh, I forgot about that."
        among the friendly
     sidewalk people
       in old rawngy nawngry
         New Orleans

                4.
           By the River

well the music
      the days, the nights
      the neighborhoods
   Faubourg Marigny
   Faubourg Treme
        got to get me
   a Faubourg Marigny

50

              hat today
        or tomorrow
after po' boy
or muffaletta
walking on the levee
above the Mississippi
        rolling down
          flowing down
foaming rippling down
          past Nawlins
  curving snaking
  raunching taking
        swamping cutting
  all along all down
      to the gulf
          to the Gulf
              o' Mexico

North Beach

maybe it's the most beautiful day of the year so far

the sun is shining

you've just ridden a bike

across the Golden Gate Bridge

and you're sitting in Washington Square Park

in the city of the gentle saint

drinking your first beer in five days

a wonderful delicious bottle

of Sierra Nevada Pale Ale

pretty girls share a green park bench with you

and even prettier girls

in black dresses and fishnet stockings

lounge on the grass in front of you

pigeons flutter

old Chinese and Japanese ladies walk by

guys on bicycles stop and eat slices of pizza

and big sandwiches

a couple walks by with a brand new baby

in a brand new baby carriage

and the pigeons and Chinese

and Japanese ladies coo

men in orange vests on big scaffolding

work on the façade

of the Church of Saints Peter and Paul

off of Corso Cristofo Columbo

just up from Joe Dimaggio

Playground and Pool

just down from City Lights Books

you have a final pull on your beer

commune with a pigeon

muse awhile

watch more pretty girls walk by

and as you leave the park

behind a guy with an umbrella talking to himself

a lady smiles

bells in the church start to chime

the statue of Benjamin Franklin winks at you

and it really is

the most beautiful day of the year

so far

Toast and Jam with Charley
Fearneyhough at Lake Tahoe

"Charley, " I said, "I'm gonna hitchhike to Denver.
I gotta see this girl there. I'm in love."

Charley said, "Dan, I'll give you a ride to the
highway."

But Charley and I both rode with Stuart Alexander
and Tom Murdock to St. Louis. And from St. Louis we
hitched west.

In Denver we couldn't find my girl.
She had moved to Idaho or somewhere.
We walked the midnight streets.
We hitched on.

In Rock Springs, Wyoming we nearly froze to death.
Middle of July, low 30s, we slept out
in a public park, no sleeping bags.
We survived.
We hitched on,
63 rides in all.

One bright morning out of Carson City, Nevada
we hitched a ride to Lake Tahoe.
I had never seen anything so beautiful.

Charley said, "Dan! Are you seeing what I'm
seeing?!?"
I said, "Yeah!"

We got dropped off.
We walked.
We got hungry.
We stopped for breakfast at a brand new inn
overlooking the clear amazing mountain lake.
We ordered eggs and bacon,
potatoes, toast and jam
that vivid summer morning
40 years ago.

My God, Charley, my God!
That toast with jam
was the best thing
I have ever tasted.

Two Brand New

So small
at first I thought
they were jackrabbits,
the two brand new
baby deer
walked with their mother
in the tall grass
across the road.

I had seen her
the night before.
She looked fat.
It crossed my mind
she could be pregnant,
but it seemed late
in the year,
the first of May.

This morning though,
there they were,—
so beautiful
there are no words—
two perfect, small,
delicate creatures.
So beautiful, so—
beautiful.

The doe walked
and grazed.
The fawns
walked with her,
their very gait
a gambol.
It must be innate,
a way to kickstart
mammal muscles,
get the kinks out.

The fawns
didn't graze,
rarely even
nudged their
mother for milk—
so young,
so fresh,
the whole world new.

I watched in wonder,
feeling blessed, lucky.
The doe and fawns
walked through our meadow
and up the hillside
behind the house
disappearing finally
into the trees and brush.

How beautiful were those baby deer?
Mary and I just built
an orchard fence,
at some expense
of time, sweat, cash, patience,
to keep the deer away
from our tender fruit trees.
If those two baby deer
wanted to graze
in our orchard,
I would gladly
open the gate
and invite them in.

Field of Budges

On warm sunny spring days
The many California poppies in our field
Open their orange blossoms
In a heartening show
Of the abundance and beauty of life.

I mow the field,
Otherwise we'd have tall grass and weeds,
Vines and wildflowers out of control.
But I mow around the poppies.
I can't bring myself to cut them down.

Yesterday we went walking in the field,
My cousins BJ and Sara, Sara's little daughter
Elizabeth, my sister Paula, Mary, Nate and I.
Elizabeth loved the swaying golden poppies.
She plucked blossoms and handed them around.

"Poppies," we told her, "these are poppies."
"Budges," she replied.
"Poppies," we insisted.
"Budges," she agreed.
So, we gave in. "Budges!"

You should have seen Elizabeth among the budges,
Her head not much higher than the blooms,
Her soft brown hair, her child's delight.

How could we deny her "budges"?
We knew what they were called
Because we had always called them by that name.
Elizabeth, seeing only what was really there,
Named them budges, and budges they became.

Win Some, Lose Some

The night I spent the night in jail, I left Gerstle's Place, 1 A.M., to hitchhike to my sister's house and watch U of L play basketball on tv. The Great Alaska Shootout. I was carrying one of those oil-can-sized 22-ounce Foster's Lagers. I had already opened it. I was walking and hitching when the cop pulled over—Officer Diggs, Figgs, something like that. "Pour out that beer," was the first thing he said.

"Oh, man, I just opened it."

"Pour it out."

"Okay."

"You know it's against the law to hitchhike," he said.

I didn't think, just blurted out, "It's not against the law to hitchhike." That was all it took. He threw me up against the car, slapped on the cuffs, shoved me into the backseat, got in and started driving.

All the way downtown I complained, pleaded and wheedled, to no avail. At the jail under the courthouse I was booked, fingerprinted and photographed.

"What'd you do, piss off a cop?" the friendly fingerprint man asked me.

"Yeah, I guess."

Next it was into the holding cell with all the other Friday night drunks. I used my one phone call to call my sister, but no one there could offer any help. "Hang in there," they told me.

Then to the regular all-night drunk tank, but not before we had to strip and spread our cheeks. "I don't play that," one old dude informed the guard, who responded, "You want a piece of me?"

"Shit, buncha faggots," the old dude grumbled, but he spread. We all did.

In the drunk tank everybody flopped out. I couldn't sleep. Oh, but first they issued cigarettes all around. What a nightmare! I've never been a smoker. One guy fell asleep with a Camel burning between his fingers. It burned almost all the way down. I grabbed it away, thinking to keep him from getting burned. That woke him up. "Smoke your own," he growled.

At 6 A.M. I was released.

"Don't let me see you here again," warned the guard.

"I don't intend to."

"Arraignment's at eight."

"Okay."

I walked the cold downtown Louisville streets till then, made my appearance, got a court date set, and limped on home.

In Anchorage, Alaska, U of L lost to N. C. State, 72-66. The next year they won their first National Championship.

How I Helped the Duke Blue Devils
Win the 1992 NCAA Division I
Men's Basketball Championship

When Duke's second NCAA basketball championship in as many years is mentioned, the names that usually leap to mind, after Krzyzewski, are Laettner, Hurley and Hill. And rightly so. Undoubtedly they all played significant roles. But there are thousands of other individuals, each of whom knows in his or her heart of hearts, that without her (or his) all-important personal contribution the championship could not have been won.

In my case it goes back to 1970, the year I entered Duke as a freshman and started preparing to face the strange new world of the latter years of the American Century. The fortunes of Duke basketball were on the wane during my four years there. Vic Bubas, who took Duke to Final Fours in 1963, '64 and '66, had retired to a vice-presidency, and his assistant coach Bucky Waters had been brought in as his replacement. This was a mistake, as we were all to learn. At times the ridiculous vicissitudes of Buckyball still haunt those of us who frequented the Indoor Stadium in the early '70s.

My freshman year, Duke still had a few leftover Bubas recruits, like Randy Denton, who later played in the ABA, and Dick DeVenzio, a P. A. announcer's dream, who later went "dribbling for drugs" in Italy (you could look it up), and Rick Katherman, whose misfortune it was to play before the era of the 3-point shot. When he got hot he could hit 25-footers all night.

But it didn't take Waters long to ruin a good program, and by my junior year he had alienated and lost all but one player, Gary Melchionni, from a freshman team that had gone 16-0. (This was in the tough ACC freshman league, in the days when frosh were not eligible for varsity play.)

In passing, I should mention that you could always get into games in those days simply by strolling over to the Indoor Stadium shortly before tip-off time—no three-night campout required. And Bucky's assistant coach, Hubie Brown, later of the New York Knicks, Atlanta Hawks, et al., was a colorful guy who taught dorm seminars in the use of forearm as attention getter in a friendly game of hoops. And we saw some great teams come through: Lefty Driesell's Maryland, with Len Elmore, Tom McMillen and John Lucas; Dean Smith's UNC with Bob McAdoo, George Karl and Walter Davis; and the Norm Sloan coached NC State team of David Thompson, Tommy Burleson and Monte Towe that beat UCLA to win the National Championship in 1974.

We loved to hate those teams, and had special cheers for them, like, "If you can't go to college, go to State" and the indispensable, "Go to hell, Carolina, go to hell." And we got to see Melchionni go off for 39 points in a win over Maryland, reportedly while under the influence of our performance-enhancing drug of choice in those days, marijuana.

Also we had Freddy, the genius cheerleader, who loved to lead us in the immortal cheer, "Harass them, harass them, make them relinquish the ball," and its football counterpart, "Maim them, maim them, strew the field with intestinal gore." At halftime Freddy would shoot and make free throws while lying on his back with his legs crossed behind his neck. He had to be handed the ball and spun into position by assistant cheerleaders.

So things were not all bad during the lean years for Duke basketball. Still, one likes to finish with the scoreboard numbers in one's favor, and enjoy the band's final spirited playing of "Devil with a Blue Dress" and the heavy on the wanh-wahs version of "Nah, nah, nah , nah, goodnight."

Happily, the fortunes of Duke basketball—mysteriously? coincidentally?—again went on the upswing shortly after Bucky Waters' departure.

FLASH FORWARD. The 1992 NCAA Men's Division I Basketball Championship. Duke vs.

Michigan. In a strategic last-minute move I decide to forego the running and bike riding ritual which has helped get us this far, and opt for watering my entire yard and garden. Admittedly it's a chancy move. The running and bike riding had done the trick for the Kentucky and the Indiana games, though just barely in the former case. I helped Duke win that one, not only by running three good miles and then riding my bike past the front door of Chico's Bidwell Mansion, which reminds me of my old Southgate dorm at Duke, but also by actually going in to work during the game, though basket-casedly running upstairs and down, watching the game haphazardly on the tv in the basement, secure in the knowledge that I was taping it at home. (I still have that tape, by the way, if any of you UK fans care to see the Christian Laettner shot one more time.) And—the big one—I went door to door collecting for the American Heart Association that morning.

All of these activities undoubtedly helped. But for the championship game against Michigan, I determined to be bold, and so watered the old homestead, as I said. It took about an hour and a half. And it worked! It's gratifying to know I made the right decision and helped the team win.

Hey, and I heard the final three minutes called by Caywood Ledford on CBS radio in his final game. Flashback to listening to Caywood call the games of the great Adolph Rupp teams of the

1960s—Cotton Nash, Louie Dampier, Pat Riley, et al.—as I grew up shooting hoops on my Kentucky backyard dirt court. Later, when cut from my high school freshman team, I kept practicing, dreaming that Rupp would drive by, see me sinking shot after shot, and invite me to try out for Rupp's Runts. That was 1966, the year Thad Jarascz made third team All-American and Wes Unseld only made Honorable Mention.

But I digress. Back to the wonderful Duke over Michigan by 20 reality. With Grant Hill coming on strong. Just as I expected. And predicted. Dook! Two in a row! Peace sign! We did know about that during my days on campus.

> Two in a row?
> Will there be mo'?
> How should I know?

Okay, if you want to know the truth . . . last year, 1991, after Duke won the championship for the first time, I went in to work the next morning, and while casually shooting wadded-up balls of scrap paper toward a wastebasket a considerable distance away, I said, "However many of these I make in a row, that's how many championships Duke is going to win." And I made seven in a row! No lie. Tom Gascoyne can vouch for this. He was there. Or else I told him about it. Anyway, it's true.

Gear and Clothing at the Ironman Triathlon
by Elwood Duke, Special Correspondent

*"When you're runnin' down my country, hoss,
You're walkin' on the fightin' side of me."*

Merle Haggard coming over the radio in the Ocean View Inn, Kailua-Kona, Hawaii. Mai Tai and I sip our coffee and chew chunks of pineapple. Our waffles and eggs should be ready soon. Through a big picture window we watch 900 people in orange bathing caps hurl themselves like lemmings into the sea. In a last-second fuck-up the Coast Guard tows a boat into their path, so that many flounder and flail in their attempt to negotiate this 2.4-mile ocean swim, the first leg of the Ironman Triathlon.

Yes, folks, this is it, the Big Event this tourist town has been gearing up for all year. The geeks are finally in the water and about ten hours from now we'll have a winner. This is the ABC/ Budweiser Light Kona Coast Ironman Triathlon World Championship, the Super Bowl of endurance sports. This is the one where the girl shat herself on national TV.

"Naked, beach-roving wretches, destitute even of rice."
—Tasman's Journal

How I ended up here, what this has to do with anything, and why seemingly sane people would choose to spend a lovely Saturday torturing themselves under a tropical sun is anybody's guess. But, as the man says, "These are strange times."

Indeed. And not likely to get less strange any time soon.

Another sip of coffee, another chunk of pineapple. It's starting to come back to me.

I came over here to the Big Island to relax. That's it. Needed to get away from the hectic pace on Maui. I met Mai Tai at the nude beach next to the Honokohau small boat harbor. She was a friendly native girl, "fertile in invention and elastic in conscience," as Twain would say. She agreed to show me around the island.

"Let's keep it simple, " I told her. "I came here for a rest."

"Otay," she replied.

As the Kona Coffee Festival parade marched into Kailua—less than 24 hours to splash-in, grossly in-shape people visible everywhere—we headed for Kilauea, an active volcano that had last erupted five days ago.

"Not to worry, " said Mai Tai, "Pele [the volcano deity] is a friendly goddess.

While exploring the countryside near the crater, noted for its fire-pits and deep earth cracks, we happened to meet some friendly people, some . . . farmers. And, this being the season of the harvest, we were invited to share and partake in the bounty of the land. An offer we couldn't refuse, as it were. Right. When the going gets weird, the weird grow vegetables, or herbs, as the case may be.

After several . . . tastes . . . of the . . . produce, one of the farmers revealed that he was also a chemist. He called himself Merlin. Merlin produced a vial of crystals. They looked and tasted a bit like salt. We found them to be very stimulating.

"These are disoxyn crystals," Merlin explained, "the crystal of crystal methedrine."

After another hour of feasting on disoxyn crystals, Ka-'u buds, and Kona coffee we decided to head for Hilo and check out the lush eastern side of the island. Merlin pointed to the red Mercury Zephyr I had rented at the airport. "Not a bad car," quoth he.

"Care to drive?" I asked

"Let's roll," he said.

We cruised east past recent lava flows, then north along the Hilo coast. We drank a few beers along the way, and smoked more pakalolo. But no more disoxyn crystals. Enough is enough. No more till at least . . . later on.

Later on can come early in the islands. Before we knew it midnight was at hand. We were seated in the lounge of the Hilo Hukilau Hotel slurping strong drinks from tall glasses.

"Let's drive back to Kona for the triathlon," I suggested.

"What for you wanna do that?" Mai Tai wanted to know. "Those people are crazy, nuts, flippo."

"Yeah, you're right," I agreed, "but crazy people fascinate me."

Now wait a minute—

This story seems to be assuming a somewhat pejorative attitude toward the Ironman Triathlon. After all, triathlon is the fastest growing sport in the world. There are those who claim that training for and competing in a triathlon is the true path to serenity, longevity and all that is good in life. Here on the Big Island there are folks who swear that Jesus is the number one triathlete. And he's coming soon. Yes. You know you've always got the number one triathlete by your side. So let's get a grip on this "story."

How 'bout it, Merle? Is the best of the free life behind us now? Are the good times really over for good? Hell, I'm just a simple hillbilly. What do I know about these things? Can you help me out here, Merle? Can you sing me back home?

But that's not Merle Haggard that Merlin has blasting on the car radio now. It's some kind of quintessential surf tune. The crazy laugh, the electric guitar. I've got it. They're playing our song— "Wipeout!"

"A little more disoxyn, Merlin, if you please."

We headed north, then west across the island, and arrived in Kailua in time for breakfast and the big splash-in. After breakfast we checked in to the Kona Seaside Hotel. I opened a beer, lit a joint, and switched on the TV.

The first swimmers started getting out of the water about an hour later. From the balcony of our room we could see the big Budweiser Light can down on the pier and hear the announcer say things like, "This geek is getting out of the water. It looks like number . . . 852. He's getting on his bicycle. He's barfing. He's turning blue. Let's give him a big hand!"

I cranked up the air conditioner, took off my clothes and got into bed with Mai Tai.

> *"Is it perfume from a dress*
> *That makes me so digress?"*
> *—T. S. Eliot*

Around noon I woke up feeling pretty good. The first triathletes would be completing their 112-

mile bike ride within an hour. Mai Tai was still snoozing. I decided to wander down to the Kona Surf hotel and watch the transition from bicycling to running. It was a hot day but the half-mile walk felt okay. As I walked I wondered, *Good God, why are these people doing this?!?*

"The first thing you have to do is get your mind around the triathlon," a guy in a Kauai Marathon t-shirt explained to me. "I haven't done that yet. That's why I'm just watching."

Well, yeah, I think I see what he means. Mountain climbers can answer their "why?" with "because it's there." But the triathlon isn't really there. Some guy in Honolulu thought it up in 1977. Maybe it's one of the symptoms of Island Fever.

But I wax philosophical, and digress.

Ah, what the hell? Might as well digress further and wax psychological. I can't help wondering what Sigmund Freud would say if he could be here for this event. "Und vhat have we here? Zee mass hysteria phenomenon? Ach! So many new patients. I'll raise zee rates."

Indeed. It is rather curious—scantily clad men and women exerting themselves strenuously, breathing hard and sweating, in something called the "ironman" competition. You don't have to be Freud to figure that out.

Well shucks, all truths wait in all things, the sages say. How does Buckminster Fuller put it? "The less people know about how sausages and laws are made, the better they will sleep at night."

No, no, Bismarck said that. What about, "Truth is visible only to eyes unclouded by longing?"

No, I think Baba Louie said that. How about, "We would be on a mission from God, if there was a God?"

Holy Mother of Babbling Bullshit! I'm getting off track. I know I've got it here somewhere. Here it is. Bucky Fuller says: "Evolution is methodically synergetic and omnimeaningful." That's it. That must be why these people are doing this.

When I got to the Kona Surf the leaders were finishing the bike ride. By the time I strolled back to town the first place guy was in the sixth mile of his marathon and looking plenty tired. Merlin and Mai Tai met me in town. We decided to hold our own Bud Light competition. Who can drink the most Bud Light before the first guy finishes? That was the best idea I had heard since the suck-the-keg contest at Tom Murdock's wedding.

The rest of that day is pretty fuzzy in my memory. I remember dancing to the tunes of the Peggy Barnes Band. They were good, playing "My Little Runaway" and "Hey Do Run Run" as the triathletes plodded toward the finish line. I remember watching baseball on TV at Don Drysdale's Club 54. And I remember being kicked off the grounds of the King Kamehameha Museum for "smoking dope," as one of the members of the Ladies Auxiliary succinctly put it.

"Our way was Northward on the naked lava."
    —*Stevenson*

Sometime after dark I awoke in the back seat of the Zephyr. Merlin was driving toward the airport. Mai Tai was passed out beside me. The highway was lined with slow moving vehicles, and along the sides of the road were hundreds of runners wearing little reflectors. I opened my window and started shouting, "Stop it! This is dangerous! Someone could get killed!"

Some of the runners had almost 20 miles to go. Many were walking. They all looked terrible. The top finishers were already in the massage room. Amidst applause and accolades they had made it to the bright TV lights and the big Bud Light can on the pier. But Great Gatsby! Out here on the insane, dangerous, jangled edge of the "competition" people were risking their lives. For what?!? "Give it up!" I kept yelling at them. But these people were beyond reach.

What's that? Who won?!? You want to know who won?!? Did you expect me to report this event with the relentless zeal and ratbastard accuracy of some half-bright, low-rent, booze-addled sportswriter?!?

Nobody won! There are no winners! This is merely another symptom, another barometer measuring the bent and twisted tenor of the times, another manifestation of the great malaise. From which there is no escape. We're all doomed and we know it. There is nowhere to run and nowhere to hide. But run. By all means run. And swim and bike if you feel like it. "Whatever gets you through the night," as the little Liverpudlian put it. You go your way and I'll go mine. Most likely. A beer and a joint for this old boy. And something stronger if you've got it.

I opened another can of Budweiser and lit a joint. Mai Tai whimpered softly in her sleep. Merlin aimed the Zephyr out through the lava lands. We were bound for other shores.

The Day Sister Jovena Wrote FUCK
on the Blackboard

First of all, I wasn't there. I was next door in the other sixth-grade classroom, Mrs. Fresno's class. So I can't vouch for the truth of everything in this story. But I'll tell it the way I heard it, right after school that day, excitedly, from Joe Coughlin, who *was* there.

"You won't believe what happened in our class today. We come in after lunch recess, right? And Sister Jovena says, kind of stern, 'Boys and girls, put your heads down on your desks and close your eyes.'

"So we're all wondering, what's this about, but we do it and we hear what sounds like her writing something on the blackboard. It doesn't take long, maybe half a minute, then it's real silent and all you can hear is breathing and I'm sitting there hoping somebody farts but I don't want to be the one. She leaves us like that for a good two or three minutes, then she says, 'All right, boys and girls, open your eyes and sit up.'

"So we sit up and there on the board is just one word, in big capital letters, F-U-C-K. Oh my God! Yes! No! We couldn't believe it, but there it was. I thought I was in some crazy dream. FUCK. Right there on the blackboard, and I thought, *My God, Sister Jovena has gone around the bend. Off her rocker. Crazy. Flipped. Loony. They're coming to take her away, ha-ha.*

"Then she says—listen to this—she says, 'Who knows what this word means?' Like it's a vocabulary quiz or something. Can you believe it? 'Who knows what this word means?' she says. 'Raise your hands.'

"Hey, even the eager beaver hand raisers like Mary Beth Timmons were not gonna swing their ugly arms around to be first on that one. No way. My God. We were all in a state of shock, trying not to laugh, not knowing what to do. Everybody was afraid to look at anybody or make a sound. You think any hands went up? No way.

"So she gets specific, singling out only boys of course, no girls. 'Tony Koren, do you know what this word means?'

" 'No, S'ter,' he mumbles.

" 'What's that, Tony? I couldn't hear you.'

" 'No, S'ter,' he mumbles a little louder.

" 'Tom Smith, have you ever seen this word before?'

" 'No, S'ter,' he says, loud enough to be heard.

"It goes on like that for five or six guys. I was dreading it but I knew she'd get to me sooner or later. 'Joe Coughlin, do you know what this word means?'

" 'No, S'ter," I say. And then real quiet, 'Do you?'

" 'What did you say?' she yells at me.

" 'No, S'ter,' I say. Mr. Innocent. So she glares at me but lets it go.

"And then she goes into this long silence, everybody nervous as hell, looking around the room and out the windows and peeking a look at the blackboard now and then, that big FUCK still up there in white chalk like the writing on the wall in that Bible story. And everybody still trying not to look at anybody and kind of feeling like running out of the room laughing like madmen, but everybody just breathing real quiet and afraid to move.

"Finally, and I mean it seemed like forever, she says, 'Boys and girls, this word that you see up here on the blackboard was found written on the brick wall outside just a little while ago. The only time it could have been written there was during our lunch recess. Now, I know that some of you know this word. And I am very sure that the boy who wrote it on the school wall is in this classroom right now, acting like a coward, making the whole class suffer because he will not admit what he did. So, I guess Father Broderick will have to hear about this, and Father Reedy, and Father Thibault. And they will talk to you boys. Girls, I am very sorry you had to be part of this. I'm quite sure none of you is the guilty party. But the guilty one will be found out, and punished. I may not know who you are, and the good boys and girls in this class may not know who you are. But God knows who you are, because He is everywhere and He sees everything. And He is very disappointed in you. I strongly advise you to go to confession as soon as possible. You are in a state of sin and your immortal soul is in danger of eternal damnation.'

"Man, she was pulling out all the big guns. She paused, and took a deep breath and kind of sighed like she was the saddest nun in the whole world, and then she says, 'Now, get out your math books.'

"You never saw such hustling and rushing to open math books. And that was it. She erased the big FUCK and we got on with afternoon classes. God only knows what'll happen tomorrow."

Hitching On

We woke up early at Kevin's. "Can I help you?" I said, or something like that in the middle of a dream.

Kevin was already up fixing his lunch. "Time to wake up, Ben," he said.

I couldn't believe it. It was still dark outside. But I got up, dressed, and pretty soon we were bouncing down the road to Port Royal. Kevin let me out in front of the general store and told me to come back and stay awhile if I wanted to cut tobacco.

Kevin headed to New Castle to meet his carpenter crew and carpool to a job in Louisville. I walked through Port Royal and down the hill toward the river. There were very few cars on the road. It was still only 6:30 or so. I was thinking about old Jack.

After about a mile I came to an overlook and there was Wendell Berry's place and Wendell's cows and the beautiful Kentucky River on its leisurely way to the Ohio. I looked over and overlooked, meditated and peed. And I agreed with old Wendell and old Kevin that Henry County was a mighty nice place.

A car pulled over and the driver offered me a ride. He was a good old boy, smoking a joint on his way to work. He offered me a hit but I declined. Too early for me. Coffee was on my mind, a good cafe in

83

Carrollton or somewhere. I told him of my plan to hitch U.S. 42, so we crossed Interstate 71 and he dropped me in Prestonville, a very small town just across the Kentucky River from the bigger town of Carrollton. I thanked him for the ride and walked across the river bridge, watching the Kentucky flow into the Ohio.

Carrollton was a sleepy southern town with three-story redbrick houses and a public square and river vistas conjuring Mark Twain's America. At the edge of town was a restaurant, the Carrollton Diner. I went in, sat down and ordered an omelet and a cup of coffee. There was an interesting 8 A.M. assortment of people in the restaurant—farmers, salesmen, old men and ladies—all gossiping over coffee. My food arrived and I ate slowly. My stomach was a bit delicate after three days of nothing but whole grains at Kevin's. But the food went down okay. I paid and left a tip, hoisted my pack and walked out of town a ways to hitch.

Quite a few cars were on the road by now but no one stopped for me for at least half an hour. Then a good old boy in a pickup pulled over. I threw my pack in the back and got in saying, "Thanks for stoppin'. Where ya headin'?"

"Going about eight miles up the road to Ghent." He told me he was originally from the west end of Louisville, had been living in Carrollton, and only recently moved to Ghent. On the windows of his truck were great pictures of full-masted ships that he had carved there.

Ghent was a *very* sleepy little town. I waited a long time for a ride, lazing in the shade with a fine view of the Ohio. A pretty girl walked around outside her house calling a dog. "Daisy. Here Daisy." I fell asleep leaning against my pack. When I woke up I walked over to a nearby gas station and bought a Coke. I resumed the hitch but had no luck, so I decided to start walking.

I walked a mile or two, past a big power plant. Finally a guy stopped for me, a middle-aged accountant having trouble collecting from his clients. "It's these small towns," he said, as if that somehow explained all his problems. He only took me a couple of miles before he had to turn. Right after he dropped me off an old farmer in a pickup stopped for me. I got in and he started talking, "Let you cool off for a while, anyway. Well, I tellya, I been gettin' things in shape. Gotta go in the hospital tomorrow in Lexington. I got these blood clots in my legs."

He drove me about five miles, talking all the way, just a friendly old tobacco farmer in overalls. "From where I drop you it's a half mile to Warsaw. Yessir, exactly half a mile to the courthouse. Well, you got to rest and cool off for a little while, anyway. Good luck to you."

I thanked the old man, hoisted my pack, and walked on through Warsaw. It seemed like more than half a mile to the courthouse. At the edge of town was the Bun Boy Restaurant. Hot from walking, I went in and had a glass of water and a delicious chocolate malt. Then I went back outside to hitch.

I had to wait about fifteen minutes before an old pickup braked to a stop and backed up for me. The driver was a strange Bonnie-and-Clyde behatted young man. He was the quiet sidekick to the man on the passenger side, a fat, eccentric, mustachioed man with a case of cold Red, White and Blue beer at his feet. I sat in the middle and we rolled on. For the first time, U.S. 42 diverged from the river and headed into some gentle hills. We stopped at a little crossroads where the fat guy, Fiddlin' Dick, owned the store. He had a lot of early model cars sitting around. The driver was his mechanic and helper. They had just come back from the Muzzle Loaders Convention up in Friendship, Indiana, to work on a car. I thanked them for the ride.

"Nothin' to it," said Fiddlin' Dick. "Here, take a couple of beers for the road."

I thanked him again and walked on a ways till I found a shady place to hitch. After an hour or more I decided to walk awhile just to find a new spot. Around the next bend a car stopped for me and I got in.

"Now where the hell are you goin', walkin' out here?" asked the driver. He was a car salesman from Warsaw, on his way to Florence to buy some cars. We talked as we rolled along.

When we got to Florence he dropped me near an on-ramp for I-75. Getting nearer to Cincinnati now, I figured I'd have better luck hitching the Interstate. Also, the sky was threatening rain and I was hoping to avoid getting caught in a downpour. I stuck out my thumb and in no time at all I had a ride into Covington in the back of a pickup. A young guy and pretty girl were up front. They dropped me in town at 3 o'clock, just before it rained. I went into a place called the Bridge Cafe to have a beer and wait out the rain. The Bridge was a strange low-life bar with odd old black and white characters lounging about and an incredible assortment of whiskeys stacked all the way to the ceiling on shelves behind the bar, with a ladder to reach the higher shelves.

After about half an hour the rain let up and I walked across the bridge to Cincinnati and on up to Fountain Square feeling good, swinging into town singing "Ramblin' Round." I found a phone and called my brother, Jim. He said he would be off work a little after five and meet me at the fountain. I waited near the fountain and watched the local scene—pretty girls walking by, a tv crew filming with their mini-cam, busses going by taking people home from work. I drifted off to sleep.

"Wake up!" someone yelled at me. I guess they couldn't stand to see someone so peaceful. It was almost five anyway. Jim showed up and we happily shook hands, he in his three-piece suit, I in my jeans and t-shirt. We walked down to where his car was parked, near Riverfront Stadium. From there we drove to the University of Cincinnati and picked up his wife, Julie, from work. Next we picked up their daughter, Mona, at afterschool daycare, and then drove home to their apartment.

I had a beer and a great and much-needed shower and shave. Jim cooked a delicious dinner of chicken, broccoli and blueberry muffins. We spent the evening watching *Heroes of Rock 'n Roll* on tv, caught the baseball scores (the Reds lost), and went to bed.

The next morning I woke up early feeling good. Jim was already up. Everybody got ready and we piled into the car. Mona went to school, Julie to work, Jim to work, and I went my way, to the highway. Jim dropped me at a good spot on I-71, near a bridge, and I stood there singing:

I've got a feeling, something that I can't explain,
Like dancing naked in that high hill country rain.

Poetry: Using Words to Express Something That Is Not Easy to Express in Words

Was that a bluebird flying?
A sword splitting a watermelon in the air?
A spring day I wrote a haiku
My head like vanilla ice cream
How nice I got a mug of water too
With a lot of audience watching me
My head feels LOVE
Relaxing is bliss LOVE
Question mark Question Mark
Like an axe
Like a piece of wood
Like a piece of wood being split by an axe
Clouds like vanilla
Clouds like ice cream
Clouds like my head like vanilla
Ice cream being split by an axe
Like a watermelon being split
By a bliss LOVE sword in the air
On a spring day with bluebirds
Flying in clouds of
Teachers standing students sitting
Pencils flying all in bliss LOVE
Ocean blueness basketball silence
Audience watching eyelids meet
Watching audience ocean enjoyable
Silent class playing basketball

Who's passing who's shooting
Who's reading who's listening
Read slowly read wheat
How does your head feel?

The *Above Average* Rocked at Its Moorings

This happened down in the Florida Keys in the spring of 1980. Annie and I had hitched down there by way of Fort Meyers where we stayed a few days with Jane Dolan. Jane was working full time on her golf game, with thoughts of turning pro. This was a surprise to us. We had known her in Louisville as just another one of the gang—going to school, partying, hanging out. But here she was in Florida with a golf coach, using lots of sunblock and spending seven hours a day on the course. I think the idea was that her rich daddy back in Kentucky would pay her expenses if she got good enough to go on the women's tour.

While Jane chipped and putted we borrowed her car and drove out to Sanibel Island where we found a nude beach and a couple of good bars—Timmy's Nook and The Mucky Duck—and went hiking at the Ding Darling Wildlife Refuge. In the evenings, back in Fort Meyers, we made big chef's salads and spaghetti suppers and went swimming with Jean at her apartment pool.

To tell the truth I don't remember how we got down to the Keys. We had tripped on acid one day out on Sanibel so maybe I was still in a purple haze. I guess we hitched across the Tamiami Trail and then I remember getting a good ride in a white

Cadillac with "Shirley T. from Big Pine Key" and her driver, John. With them we stopped at just about every bar and roadhouse between Miami and Big Pine Key, so there's something else that may have contributed to my lack of vivid memory.

Anyway, we hitched on down to Key West and stayed several days at the Eden House. We hit the bars and beaches, drank rum coladas, ate fish and black beans, toured Ernest Hemingway's old home and met the eight and nine-toed supposed descendants of his cats. Not a bad stay. We spent most of the money we had made working in Louisville. Our plan was to hitch to New Orleans, stay with Greer and Crawfish, and try to find work there for a month or so. We hitched out of Key West on a Tuesday afternoon.

"Your penis is sticking out of your shorts," said Annie.

"That's not my penis, it's my balls."

"Well, whatever it is, stick it back in there."

"Okay."

A white Ford van pulled over. We ran up and looked in.

"Chico, man," said the driver.

"Ben, man," I said.

"Annie," said Annie.

We got in and Chico took off driving like a madman.

"Puerto Rico, man," he said.

"Kentucky, man," I said.

"Pennsylvania," said Annie.

"Got any mota, man?" asked Chico.

"Si."

Annie rolled a joint and we passed it around. This mellowed Chico out a bit and he slowed down to a less frightening speed.

Chico wasn't going very far but he got us up to Boca Chica where we hitched a good ride with a friendly blonde girl in a little Datsun pickup. Her name was Jenny.

"You know it's against the law to hitchhike down here?" Jenny asked.

"Yeah, we heard something about that."

"Just in this county, Monroe County. After the big hippie invasion of the sixties they passed all these laws—no hitchhiking, and no camping except in authorized campgrounds. The cops really enforce it too."

Just then—we happened to be near a campground entrance—she braked and pulled over to pick up another hitchhiker. He looked in the window, and said, with a German accent, "Hi. I am Johann. This camping is full. Can you take me to the next camping."

"Sure. Climb in the back," said Jenny.

Johann climbed in and we took off again.

"Y'all want some beer?" asked Jenny.

"Sure. Why not?"

At the next convenience store she stopped and got a twelve-pack. We broke out the beer and passed one back to Johann. It was twenty miles to the next campground. Jenny drove in and checked it out. But it was full, too. At the exit we picked up another hitchhiker, Brad from Vermont.

"Hop in and have a beer," said Jenny.

We rolled along.

"I tell you what," said Jenny, "it's gonna be dark in a couple of hours and you all are gonna be in a fix cause there's no more campgrounds. Maybe you could stay at my place."

"All of us?" asked Annie.

"Yeah. Except my husband, Larry, he might not like it. He's kind of real jealous and kind of, you know, violent. But here's what we could do. We could tell him you're an old friend of mine that I happened to run into down in Boca Chica, and that these are all friends of yours. That should make it okay."

This didn't sound like too good of a plan to me, and I said so. Jenny lived on Marathon Key, so eventually it was decided that she would drop us at the Seven Mile Grille just across the Seven Mile Bridge on Marathon, then she would go home and talk to Larry, and if things were cool she would come back and get us.

That was the last we saw of Jenny. Brad and Johann and Mary and I sat down at the Seven Mile

Grille and ordered a pitcher of beer. After a while we ordered chili dogs and grouper chowder, and another pitcher of beer. We started talking to a guy named Curt who told us he was the mate of a fishing boat. He pointed it out to us in the small boat harbor next to the grill. His day's work done, he was adjusting his attitude before heading home. Several pitchers later he took off. The grill was closing and it was decision time for our contingent of hitchhikers. We talked about hiking, hitching (illegally), camping (illegally), or maybe pooling our money for a motel room.

"What about that boat?" said Brad.

"What boat?" asked Johann.

"That fishing boat the mate works on. Maybe we could slip on and sleep there."

"I don't know," said Annie.

"We could have a look," I said.

The *Above Average* rocked gently at its moorings as four sloshed travellers snuck aboard. Everything was nice and quiet. Annie and Johann and I rolled out our bags near the cabin. Brad climbed to the upper deck for more air. We were just drifting off to dreamland when footsteps and flashlights roused us. It was two representatives of the Monroe County Sheriff Department. Apparently the harbormaster had seen or heard us and called them.

"My God! How many of you are there?" said the Sheriff.

We stood up and were counted.

"Byron, put all their gear in the trunk," he said to his deputy.

They frisked us and checked I.D.s.

"My God! Ford City. P. A.," said the Sheriff when he looked at Annie's license. "Girl, I'm from Greenville, P. A. Don't you know coming onto a man's boat down here is like breaking into a man's steel mill up there?"

"I tried to tell these guys."

She was right, of course. It had been a stupid thing to do. But we were drunk and tired; it had seemed like the line of least resistance. And really I think we were destined for an encounter with the forces of lawn order no matter what we did that night. So now we were bundled into the Sheriff's car and taken to the station. At least they didn't handcuff us.

At the station we were the center of attention. A group of sheriff recruits were in training and this was the perfect opportunity to instruct them in correct procedure. Our packs were brought in and Byron and the cadets were set to searching them. We were instructed to empty our pockets and surrender our belts and shoelaces.

"So we don't get desperate and hang ourselves," I told Annie.

"Yeah, I was just contemplating that," said Brad.

"Hush up now," said the Sheriff. "Come on over here by my desk and we'll get the paperwork done. Byron, phone the boat owner and see if he wants to press charges."

The Sheriff seated himself behind his typewriter and started copying down information from our IDs. Johann's German passport gave him some trouble. Johann, whose English had been pretty good all day, had apparently decided that being an ignorant foreigner would be his best defense. So when the Sheriff said—"Johann, it says here you're seventy centimeters tall. What's that mean?"—Johann replied, "I not understand."

Annie, for some reason, was now tacitly appointed his interpreter. The Sheriff looked at her appealingly. "Looks like about six feet tall," she said.

"Weight, thirteen stone," read the Sheriff. "How much do you weigh, Johann?"

"Yah, thirteen stone."

"What's he say?" the Sheriff asked Annie.

"Looks like about a hundred and eighty pounds," Annie said.

"Okay. Next—"

"Hey, Sheriff! Look at this!" shouted one of the cadets.

"What the hell? Can't you see I'm busy?"

"Look!"

It was a fat ounce of pot in a baggie that the cadet had just pulled from Johann's backpack.

"What the hell is this, Johann?" asked the Sheriff.

"I never see it before," said Johann.

"Do I look stupid to you, Johann?"

"Yes. I never see it before."

"What?"

"I not understand."

"Oh, Johann, I'm very disappointed in you. Do you know what prison is, Johann? Not jail, prison. What would Germany think, Johann, if I called up and told them you were in prison here in Florida?"

"I not understand," said Johann.

"He says he doesn't understand," said Annie.

Just then the boat owner walked in, a white-haired, fiftyish fisherman. He looked more tired than mad.

"Howdy, Paul," said the Sheriff.

Paul nodded. "So these are the desperadoes," he said, taking us in. "Avery, there's no damage to my boat. I'd rather not press charges."

"You sure?"

"Yeah. I'm going home to bed."

"Okay. Sorry we had to get you down here."

At this point the Sheriff actually looked a bit relieved. He knew he wasn't going to have to deal with us much longer. I don't think he really wanted to hassle with busting a German national for an ounce of pot. He and Byron would probably split it later. Our belts, shoelaces and pocket contents were returned and we were given a short lecture on the sanctity of private property and the dangers of hitchhiking.

"Now," said the Sheriff, " you have two choices. You can either walk until you're out of this county, or you can get a motel room for the night. Do not, under any circumstances, let me catch you hitchhiking, or camping anywhere other than an officially authorized campground. Do I make myself clear?"

"Yes sir, Sheriff."

"Yes."

"Yes."

"Yah."

"Okay. Now get your gear and get out of here."

We saluted the cadets and shuffled out. At a safe distance from the Sheriff Station we held a conference. The E-Z Rest Motel was just across the highway. Brad, feeling guilty that his move to the upper deck had been responsible for all our problems, volunteered to pay for a room. He walked over and rented a single for twenty bucks.

"Okay," he said, when he came back with the key. "I'll go in. You guys come in five or ten minutes."

"Are you sure this will be okay?" asked Johann. His English was returning.

"Yeah, sure. No problem."

"That's what you said about the boat."

But the room worked out fine. Brad took the bed and the rest of us slept on the floor. In the morning we left at ten-minute intervals to avoid suspicion, then regrouped at a nearby cafe where we drank coffee and talked and laughed before going our separate ways. That day Annie and I took a bus to Orlando and hitched on from there.

The Cool Coast

by the big blue
Pacific Ocean
one little bird
and me

> Mendocino
> Highway One
> surfboard towed
> by bicycle

> foggy cows graze
> summer mid-day haze

cool on the coast   Elk Cove
cows chew cuds   Are you kidding me?
and huddle   A knockout spot

foggy cool
July Mendocino   one turkey vulture
cypress trees   six brown pelicans
                                an osprey

Frog Pond road   great blue heron
Mazda turns in   wading
zoom-zoom   cries *kraak,* flies away

> Sea Ranch Golf Links
> nine deer graze
> first fairway
> golfers stalk birdies

Going To The Baths At Esalen; or
Shootout At The I'm O.K. You're O.K. Corral

I first heard of Esalen in a college psychology course in the early 1970s. Esalen by the sea. Named after an American Indian tribe. Set in mythical, magical Big Sur, California. Famous in human potential and humanistic psychology circles. Synonymous with the easygoing, tolerant California lifestyle.

A few years later Charley Fearneyhough and I passed through Big Sur on our first big hitchhiking trip out West. We saw Esalen from the road but had no real desire to visit. We were more into beer and girls and electronic ping-pong at the time. Again in 1979 I hitched through Big Sur. By then I had read Henry Miller and Hunter Thompson. Both mention hot springs at Big Sur. A fellow hitchhiker told me about the hot springs at Esalen—"Yeah, great hot baths. Free to the public late at night." I was thinking about going, but before midnight I hitched a ride with two pretty blonde girls who were going all the way to L. A. Well, what would you have done?

In December of 1980 I once again came to California, this time accompanied by my main squeeze, Mary Miller. The baths were in a corner of my mind. I thought we'd try to stop there in February on our way to L. A. Until then we were staying in Palo Alto and working temporary jobs to earn more travelling money.

Eric Crockett, an old Forest Service buddy, was living in Petaluma, California, having moved there from Eugene, Oregon to attend graduate school at Sonoma State University. His partner, Rita Moore, was visiting for the holidays. Shortly after Christmas, Eric and Rita and Mary and I decided to get together. We met in San Francisco, traipsed around Golden Gate Park, toured the Steinhart Aquarium, had tea in the Japanese Tea Garden, stopped by the Swiss Embassy and the Jungian Institute for esoteric reasons of Eric's, and then decided to drive down the coast on Highway 1.

In Pacifica we stopped for burgers at the world's nicest A & W Root Beer stand. At San Gregorio we walked on the beach and saw a great sunset. We talked things over and decided we would drive on to Big Sur and go to the baths at Esalen. Eric had been there a few years back. He said it was free after midnight.

We took our time down the coast, stopping in Santa Cruz for bookstores and beer, and in Carmel for coffee. We got to Big Sur about 11 o'clock and went to Nepenthe, the famous bar where Jack Kerouac almost met Henry Miller. At Nepenthe we shared a liter of red wine.

It must have been at Nepenthe that things started to get complicated, although I say that only in retrospect. At the time everything seemed copacetic. We were all very much looking forward to going to the baths.

I walked outside to the patio and talked to some folks around the fire. They had been reading about fusion and fission in *Omni Magazine*. One guy was optimistic about the future. Another guy, his brother, wasn't quite so sure. Eventually the conversation drifted to nude beaches and to the baths. These folks were going to Esalen, had been there before. They said they would see us there and turn us on to some dynamite reefer—Humboldt County sinsemilla. The baths opened to the public at 1 A. M., not midnight, they informed me.

At midnight or thereabouts the bar started closing. It took a while for everyone to get going. Along about 12:30 I found myself talking to a rather scraggly looking young man with a backpack. He told me he had hitched down from Alaska and that it had been his dream to go to the hot baths at Esalen. He was looking for a ride the rest of the way. I said we would give him a ride. He said, "Thanks. Would you like to smoke some purple bud?"

I said, "Sure. Can my girlfriend join us?"

He said, "Yeah."

Eric and Rita headed for the car. They seemed to be into talking to each other alone seriously. That was my perception.

The "purple bud" was outstanding. The guy with the backpack, Eddie, must have been smoking a lot of it. It took him a long time to roll one joint, and after it was lit he kept letting it go out as he told us, with frequent digressions, a story about grizzly bears at the Anchorage dump. After three hits I was plenty stoned. Mary and Eddie finished the joint. We talked a while longer and then walked down to the parking lot where several big dogs were running around wild. A lady who worked at the bar arrived on the scene and got them under control. We piled into the car with Eric and Rita and headed for Esalen.

The road seemed to have gotten a lot curvier while we were at the bar. Mary and I found it amazing and hilarious that Eric was able to keep the car on the road by continually turning the steering wheel. Eddie appeared to be in a trance. Every once in awhile he would emit what sounded like little grunts of pleasure. Rita just laughed and Eric chuckled and drove.

We arrived at Esalen and parked in the parking lot by the road. We tripped happily down the path to the baths. Signs directed us to a building where we were to check in. Eddie pulled out of his stupor and took the lead in eager anticipation of his dream come true.

We followed Eddie into a building where we encountered some official Esalen humanistic psychology types who informed us that only "locals" got in for free. For everyone else there was a five-dollar admission charge to the baths. This was the first we had heard of a five-dollar fee. Apparently it was an innovation designed to keep out the riff-raff. This presented us with a problem because we had spent almost all of our money. Apparently we were the riff-raff they were trying to keep out.

Amazingly, Eddie produced a rather dubious local connection, saying he used to camp on so-and-so's land down on such-and-such creek, and was allowed in for free. Without a local connection, and falling short of the requisite five dollars each, we appealed to their sense of fair play. Eric explained that he had been to the baths for free previously and that we had driven down from San Francisco for the express purpose of enjoying a midnight soak.

There were four guys there to collect money. Three of them were lounging about leisurely and seemed inclined to accept Eric's view of the situation. But the fourth was very upright and officious. In an English accent this guy said, "I'm sorry, but if you can't pay the required fee we can't allow you in. You're not locals."

"When did you start charging five dollars?" asked Eric.

"We've always charged, as far as I know."

"Obviously you don't know too much," said Eric. "How long have you been here?"

"That is irrelevant," said the guy.

It appeared to me that this conversation was not heading in a direction designed to get us into the baths. So I intervened.

"What's your name?" I asked the guy.

"John," he said.

"Oh, like John Lennon," I said. "John, I've hitchhiked through here several times. Sort of like the guy you just let in. The truth is we can't afford to pay five dollars each, and we really would like to go to the baths."

One of the other humanistic psychology types spoke up, "Why not let them in, John? They seem alright."

"You know as well as I do, Bruce, that the reason we are here is to collect money. If we're going to start letting every Tom, Dick and Harry in for free, we might as well be in bed sleeping."

"I didn't know you felt so strongly about it," said Bruce.

"Obviously someone has to," said John.

"Couldn't you just make an exception in our case?" asked Mary.

"Why should I?"

"Because we really don't have twenty dollars and we really would like to go in."

"Sorry," said John.

"Can I tell you something?" I asked.

"Go ahead," said John.

"The first time I hitched through here was with my best friend Charley Fearneyhough. That was about seven years ago. Last year Charley died of cancer. It would mean a lot to me if you would let us in."

"We don't need that kind of shit around here," said John.

I was very taken aback at this response. My impression had been that this was exactly the kind of shit Esalen was known for. Maybe he thought I was making it up. Eric and Rita and Mary and I decided to go back outside and regroup.

"That one guy is really unbelievable," said Mary.

"No kidding," said Eric. "Maybe we should just leave."

"I'd like to give him a poem," said Rita.

We all agreed that this couldn't hurt. Rita produced a pen and notebook and wrote a short poem. We walked back in and she handed it to John.

"What's this?" he asked.

"A poem," she said.

"I can't read this," he said, not even looking at it.

One of the other guys was curious though. He picked up the piece of paper and read aloud:

Joan Baez has written some poems;
Tom Robbins has written some books:
A hitchhiker makes the world his home;
That's the way it looks.

This sounded pretty good to me, maybe not Emily Dickinson but at least an expression that we were all in this thing together and that in certain ways everyone was a "local" of Big Sur. But John was not moved.

"Look," he said. "It is very clear to me that you are not going to get in for free."

It was at this point that in my mind I said, "Fuck it. We don't need to go to the baths at this capitalist psychology institute." I didn't say "fuck you" to John but I did fire a parting volley, raising certain questions about his parentage and his cranial capacity. Mary covered me and we all once again retreated to the outdoors.

We were just about ready to give it up and leave when John came outside to talk to us. I thought maybe we had gotten to him and he was ready to capitulate. But he gave us a sales pitch. "This is really the best hot springs deal on the entire West Coast. You can ask anyone. Or call our 24-hour toll free number and you can hear a recording describing the facilities."

I couldn't believe it. I was really ready to leave now but Eric couldn't resist engaging John in a bit more verbal give and take. He invoked Carl Rogers and his ideas about conflict resolution. "Just try to step outside your roll as money collector," Eric suggested.

"I've had enough of this," said John. "I'm giving you guys ten minutes to either pay the money or get out of here."

"Ten minutes?!?" asked Eric, incredulous.

"That's right," said John.

It was at this point that Mary commented on the obvious and said to John, "You are really a flaming asshole."

And that was the end of it. John went back inside without another word and we headed for the car. Call an asshole an asshole and get the hell out of Esalen.

We drove back up the road to Pfeiffer State Park where we found an unoccupied campsite, rolled out our sleeping bags, and Esalen Shmessalenned off to sleep.

For Mary, 25 Years and Counting

I know it hasn't always been easy
To be the one who loves me.
Lord knows we both have our faults.
But we accept them as we accept each other,
Not always easily and unconditionally,
But truly as we vowed
Twenty-five years ago
In Dog Canyon, New Mexico.
I meant what I said then
And I still mean it today:
For richer, for poorer,
In sickness and in health,
Forsaking all others,
Till death do us part.

Well, let's hope that'll still be a while.
I'll try for another twenty-five if you will.
Together we have walked and hitched
And driven our road,
In Kentucky and California and
Points beyond and in between.
With Nate added to our joy,
How could we, how can we go wrong?
Earthquake, flood—
We have survived and prospered.
Consistently, if not constantly aware
Of how lucky we are,

We give thanks.

I give thanks for you, Mary.
I love you, you know.
You always were,
You always are,
You always will be—
The Best.

Big Two-Hearted Hitchhike

Saturday night Mary and I slept in a field near the twin cinemas in Vernal, Utah. Sunday morning we woke up early and started hitching west on U.S. 40. It was a beautiful sunny morning in early summer. Birds and crickets were chirping all around.

A young guy in a late model Cordoba pulled over to give us a ride. He said he was from Ohio and had just been in Utah two weeks, working an oilrig job. He was on his way home after working the night shift. He took us about 40 miles to Roosevelt where he dropped us at a mini-mart, wished us good luck and gave us five dollars. We thanked him and used the money to buy orange juice and granola bars.

After this snack we walked back to the highway. A pickup pulled over.

"Where you heading?" asked the driver.

"Idaho," I said , "Ketchum."

"Well, I'm not going that far but I can take you up the road a ways. Hop in."

I rode in the back and Mary sat up front with the driver. He played a Grateful Dead tape and gave her a big roach to smoke. This ride took us another 40 miles or so to Duchesne, where the driver turned off to take Highway 33 South to Price. He was driving to the pick-up spot for a raft trip.

Duchesne was just a sleepy little Sunday morning Utah town. We grabbed our gear and walked to a nearby park, smoked the roach, got lazy, snuggled in the shade, swung on the swings, looked at the map, and duct taped my guitar case, which had begun to fall apart. After about an hour-and-a-half we hoisted our packs and walked to the edge of town.

It wasn't yet noon, but the day was already very hot. We hitched for a half-hour with no success, then decided it was time for more snacks. Mary sat with the packs while I walked to a nearby store. I purchased a tin of sardines, a bag of Fig Newtons, two cans of apricot nectar and two Eskimo pie ice cream bars.

When I came back we ate the ice cream bars and stashed the rest of the food in our packs. Another pickup truck pulled over. The driver was an off-duty park ranger from nearby Starvation Lake State Park. He was on his way to the lake to do a little fishing. Although it was five miles off the main road, we decided to ride along in hope of a nice place to swim.

Starvation Lake turned out to be pretty disappointing. It looked aptly named. Mary was especially bummed out. She would much rather have been snuggling in the shade than swimming in a very cold lake or sunning on a desert beach. I found the plunge refreshing, but had to admit that Starvation

Lake was not worth going out of our way. We hitched a lucky ride back to U.S. 40 with two gay men in a Jeep that had an eagle painted on the hood.

Back on the highway it didn't take long to hitch another ride. This turned out to be a good long one, a hundred miles or more. The driver was a young man named John. We rode and talked and shared a joint. John was from the Skagit Valley of Washington, where he was raised as a Mennonite. John the Anabaptist.

John had graduated from a Mennonite college in the Midwest, then taught in public schools for a few years. He had recently been back East but was now on his way back to Washington to help with the family farm. He dropped us near Park City, at the intersection of U.S. 40 and Interstate 80.

We had just waved goodbye to John when two guys in a truck pulled over. These guys were oilrig workers headed east to Rawlins, Wyoming. We caught a ride with them about 20 miles to where I-84 takes off north from I-80.

A longhaired, pot-smoking man in a VW Bug pulled over. He took us another 20 miles north. Next a couple in a Chevy van with four kayaks on top gave us a ride almost to Ogden. One more short ride with a fat man in a pickup took us to the Willard Bay exit. "Truckers call this the Fruit Loop," he told us. "Lots of orchards around here."

We thanked him for the ride and hitched a little more. The sun was setting beautifully behind the mountains. Mosquitos were thick.

"It's been a pretty good day of hitching," I said.

"Yeah," said Mary, "lots of rides and not too much waiting."

"Until now."

Just then a cop pulled into the median nearby to await speeders.

"Want to call it a day?" I asked.

"Might as well."

We walked down the ramp till we were well off the highway, found a nice grassy spot and rolled out our sleeping bags. We munched Fig Newtons and drank apricot nectar. The night was clear and cool, moon three days past full, mosquitoes subdued. We slept till bright sunny morning and got up to resume the hitch.

Monday promised to be another hot day. Hitching was good. A longhaired guy on his way to work in Logan pulled over. We threw our packs in the back of his truck and jumped in the cab. While he drove, Mary rolled a joint out of some of his roaches. It was barely lit when he had to drop us off. "Keep it," he told us. We thanked him and grabbed our packs.

A guy and girl in an old International pickup stopped.

"You don't happen to have a joint do you?" asked the guy.

"Yeah, as a matter of fact we do."

All four of us sat in the cab, smoked the joint and drank good black coffee out of a thermos. The ride ended at the Cross-X Cafe near Tremonton, Utah. We all went in and breakfasted heartily on ham, eggs, toast, hash browns, o.j. and coffee.

After breakfast Mary and I thanked the couple, walked back to the highway and hitched a ride all the way to Jerome, Idaho with a guy named Zack. While he drove Zack told us his story.

He had recently gotten out of the state prison in Boise, where he had served two years on a one to fifteen for possession of cocaine. He was only twenty-two. Said he used to make $40,000 a month dealing around Sun Valley. He said prison was really bad. Now he was just getting back on his feet. He showed us pictures of his wife and two-year-old daughter. Zack was pretty tired, having worked the graveyard shift as a welder, so he let me drive awhile. His truck was a nice little Datsun pickup. Made me wish I had one.

Around 12:30 Zack dropped us at a cafe on U.S. 93. We had a couple of beers and ate a leisurely lunch. At 2:30 we returned to the highway to hitch on in the hot sun. At 4:30 we were still waiting. At 5:30 we took a break and went back to the cafe. The thermometer out front read 92 degrees. We ordered iced tea.

While we sat at the counter, in no hurry to get back outside, two more hitchhikers showed up. One was a fat sweaty guy. He gulped a glass of water and hit the road. The other guy was covered with tattoos. He ordered a root beer and sat and talked awhile. He was an ex-Navy man on his way from Sacramento, California to Billings, Montana.

The cafe was run by a friendly old couple. It felt good to be sitting there. Through the window everyone watched the fat guy hitching. We decided to order supper. I had a cheeseburger. Mary had a salad. The fat guy got a ride and the other guy went out to hitch. Around 7 o'clock he got a ride and we went back out to give it another try.

I found a big piece of plasterboard beside the highway and made a sign that said KETCHUM. Pretty soon we had a ride as far as Shoshone with a businessman in a Pontiac Catalina. He dropped us at the edge of town. Before long the same man picked us up again and took us 50 more miles to Bellevue. His business contact in Shoshone hadn't been in.

By now it was dark. We were tired and dirty, so decided to splurge and paid 20 dollars for a motel room. It was a good room with a big shower and a color tv. I ran out and bought some beer and chips. When I came back we took a shower, drank beer, ate chips, watched tv, made love for a wonderfully long time and drifted off to sleep.

It was almost noon when we awoke. We checked out of the motel and had coffee at a nearby cafe. Then we hitched one easy ride to Ketchum with a couple in an old Mercury Comet. We walked to the Ketchum Free Public Library and did a little reading. Next we stopped by the Forest Service office to get information on campsites. After that we bought some groceries and hitched a ride out Warm Springs Road to Frenchman's Bend. There we made camp near a hot pool, cooked and ate a great spaghetti supper, and crawled contentedly into our tent.

There were plenty of days coming when we could fish the swamp.

dusk

at dusk
by the pond
on the margin
on the mystic margin
where the veil is thin
the paper thin veil
between this world
and another

at dusk
the thin veil
mystic margin
coots and buffleheads
great blue heron
rippling almost linear
reflection of bright Venus
in the water

Mayacama Song

Seven geese
New moon
Late September
Mayacamas
One dog
One ball
Old rough road

Pickin' rocks
Up off the ground
Put 'em in a
Cactus garden
Sittin' by a
Streamline trailer
Sun going down

One love
Two hearts
Three hearts
Sweetheart
Sittin' by a
Cactus garden
Late in the day

Nude beach
Trailer park
Cactus garden
Beg your pardon
Wait until the
Sun goes down

See what we see
Oak trees
Bay trees
Palm trees
Apple trees
Waitin' for the
Skunks and bats and
Foxes to come out

Waitin' for the
Little catlike
Skunks to come out

Waitin' for the
Little mothlike
Bats to come out

Waitin' for the
Little doglike
Foxes to come out

New moon
Sinkin' down
Late September
I remember
All the other
Late September
Moons that I've seen

All the other
Late September
Moons that I've seen

Seven geese
New moon
Late September
Mayacamas
One dog
One ball
Old rough road

One dog
One ball
Old rough road